The Red Dress

Mary Ann Mulhern

National Library of Canada Cataloguing in Publication

Mulhern, Mary Ann
          The red dress / Mary Ann Mulhern.

(Palm poets series ; 07)
ISBN 0-88753-379-5

1. Convents—Poetry. I. Title. II. Series.

PS8576.U415R43 2003   C811'.6   C2003-902757-0
PR9199.4.M848R43 2003

The Palm Poets Series is published by Black Moss Press at
2450 Byng Road, Windsor, Ontario N8W 3E8. Black Moss
books are distributed in Canada and the U.S. by Firefly Books,
3680 Victoria Park Ave., Willowdale, Ont. Canada. All orders
should be directed there.

Black Moss would like to acknowledge the generous support
of the Canada Council and the Ontario Arts Council for its
publishing program.

Le Conseil des Arts | The Canada Council
du Canada | for the Arts

ONTARIO ARTS COUNCIL
CONSEIL DES ARTS DE L'ONTARIO

The Red Dress

Mary Ann Mulhern

Black Moss
2003

for my parents,
Patrick and Ann,
always there.

Acknowledgments

I wish to acknowledge and thank my family and
friends who, from the beginning, listened for a *voice*
in my poetry. I especially want to express appreciation
to Marty Gervais, who *saw* this book before I did and
who edited these poems with a craft formed in art.

5

Prologue

In June 1964, I resigned from a teaching position and entered a convent. At the time, my best friend had died. I believed it was God's will for me to dedicate my life to religion and the service of others. During my eight years in community, I received the habit and took first vows, which I renewed each year for five years. I did not take final vows and left the convent in June, 1972.

Until the sixties, this way of life was unquestioned, and in many ways it facilitated the work of founding schools, hospitals, orphanages and homes for the aged. As the poem, "Sisters of the Sixties", points out, married women also had many restrictions on their lives. The sixties brought about powerful cultural, political, sexual and spiritual changes. These impacted on women both in religious and secular life.

The clause relating to *freedom of conscience* in Vatican Two allowed many women to question their way of of life and, as a result, women in convents began to leave in significant numbers. At the same time fewer women entered religious life and decided to live their lives in the context of choice and equality.

Poems in "The Red Dress", are not meant to depict any one community and actual names are not used. Some of the stories in these poems come from my own experience. Some are accounts as told by other former sisters.

Convent life, for me, was a bittersweet experience, which evokes memories of sadness, intense loneliness and guilt, as well as joy, humour and compassion. Many of the young women who entered in the sixties were intelligent, talented and beautiful. I feel that my sense of independence and continued love of study is partly due to life in community.

Religious life, as I lived it for eight years in the 1960's and early seventies, has changed. There were many good traditions and values, which remain. Nevertheless, the youngest sister in many communities is in her mid-fifties.

wildflower

an old nun
who made
wildflower wine
said
it tasted of summer
along with something
she could not name

she served her wine
in a painted cup
as I drank
I pictured her

young
dancing in sungold
fields
long hair
free of convent veils
wildflower
crushed in winter wine

castle

summer at the farm
rain filling a hollow
near the wintered barn
Colleen's father
building a rough wooden raft
carving an oar
from a fallen branch

Colleen and I
carrying water and food
making our voyage
over muddied waters
named as a river
a lake an inland sea

paddle poised
to battle demons
spying from the deep
keeping us away
from stones
rising from a moat
into castle walls
embraced in light
built in minds
too young
to doubt.

if

if my friend
Colleen
had not driven
to university
that slippery Dec. day
she would have stayed
on the farm
brought hot tea
with buttered biscuits
to her father
in the barn
offered to brush
the new mare
in her stall

Colleen
would have called me
before afternoon classes
planned Saturday shopping
talked about the new guy
in her chemistry lab

she did drive
took care around
icy bends
along snow-covered roads
to a light
turning red

another driver
couldn't brake
drove through the light
into a yellow Volks
into Colleen's
past present
future.

11

thou shalt not

fetters of blind faith
trail through my youth
long drab traces of
thou shalt not
i glimpse life through
narrow bars
pillars of religion

trespass of colour
pink turning to crimson
danger of red
my fingers longing to
touch silk folds
warm flesh covering me
whispering promises of morning
my tongue thirsting for
all the sweetness
of a mouth
that opens

12

flower

girls covering
rosebud breasts
aspiring to be nuns
climbing the hill
entering convent doors
high school without a dance
a prom dress
a goodnight kiss

pleated black uniforms
worn with a belt
letters from home
handled by strangers
envelopes torn
like flesh in a war

pretty youth
answering bells
in a desert
sweet white flower
named "Everlasting"
in a book of rules.

greeting

walking down
polished convent halls
"praise be to Jesus"
tones of greeting
as if he were here
keeping silence
in his desert of forty days

before water changed
to wine
before Mary of Magdela
bathed his feet
in silent tears
dried naked skin
in folds of golden hair
he embraced her then
so many sins
redeemed in a name
"Mary"

14

invitation to Cana

Sister Carlene
young novice-mistress
committed to sisters
"in formation"
we are your family now
we read all letters
newspapers radio television
distract from communion
with God
friendship is not
permitted here
Jesus is your friend
your savior your spouse

i've been invited
to my brother's wedding
to sing Shubert's Ave
at the Offertory
Sister Carlene explains
sisters do not attend
weddings

my brother and his bride visit
bring sweet wedding cake.

15

visiting day

last Sunday of the month
circles of hardback chairs
in a basement room
families gathering loudly
around a beloved
daughter, sister, cousin, aunt

my mother
handing me a package
toothpaste, soap, deodorant, shampoo
her voice straining worry
*"what's wrong with your skin
what are they feeding you here?"*

my father
needing a glass of water
before his long journey
home.

sisters of the sixties

visiting day
jenny sits in a circle
smiles at her younger sister
tripping over convent black

jenny holds a baby
feels another in her womb
a doctor sees a young mother
fading child after child
offers a forbidden pill

hearing her confession
the priest makes his demand
price of marriage vows
every year a son

jenny wonders
about a priest
whose meals are served
clothes are pressed
car is new
a man who never hears
a baby cry
never does without milk

maybe sister emilee
made a better choice
in her world of white
and black

something in my life

a rash begins
spreads into angry red
sister carlene
takes me aside
calls me by name
"mary, your skin
looks sore"

i feel
sister carlene's words
touching my face
like a soft hand
healing wounds
stopping tears.

she arranges for
a physician
who offers
a gentle lotion
tells me
something in my life
is gathering worry
breaking out

mending

Sister Carmella
measured brides of Christ
sewed endless bolts of black
satin in her hands

when cancer
brought her to Calvary
she touched his knotted hem
threads of blood
strands of light

these she kept
sacred in her sewing box
fed through a needle's eye,
mending.

Benedicamus Domino

in the purple silence
of Lent
we file into the refectory
smelling fresh coffee
oatmeal
homemade bread

Sister Mary Walter
places generous weight
on her stool
breaking wooden legs
leaving her in
a wrinkled heap
laughing
reverend mother
gives blessing to joy
"Benedicamus Domino"
chorus of three-hundred voices
rising like fireworks
in a summer sky
"Deo Gratias".

Benedicamus Domino — Let us bless the Lord
Deo Gratias — Thanks be to God

sacred silence

when silence is sacred
midnight till dawn
words break into
forbidden spaces
filled with trees
bearing fruit
ripe with questions

21

nightgown

rough cotton
so many yards
under which
to dress
undress

white vestment
purification
flowing over
breasts torso
hips vagina legs

shaping thought
into a shroud
for the night
and feeling desire

believing all this stuff

in the beginning
i wondered
asked questions
made judgments
when i saw
nuns in chapel
in the refectory
on their knees
loudly asking
for prayers
for one who
fails in poverty
in obedience
in charity

after six months
of no friends
no family
no free press
no answering voice

authority took me
in its teeth
like a mother cat
moving her kitten
to higher ground

on silent paws

23

romance

sister clarisse
finds silk in
coarse convent veils
romance in virginity
held in the passion
of youth
beauty
in a face
untouched by lips
movement of a body
dancing alone
rhythms from
another time
when visions spoke
when angels sang
when miracles
changed virtue
to light
shining in halos
eternal glory of saints.

feast day

reverend mother's feast day
her *benedicamus domino*
transforms the refectory
voices loosened from silence
rise

words loud greetings
bounce back and forth
between extra servings
grapefruit eggs bacon
fresh coffee cake

a painting presented
explosion of crimson
life in the marketplace
released in oil
from the hand
of a novice
with a painter's eye

name day

we are brides
long brushed hair
lace wedding veils
white satin dresses
seed pearl buttons

the bridegroom
waits at the altar
to embrace wise virgins
answering his call

ten priests concelebrate,
at the offertory
thirty young women
leave in procession
to become nuns

scissors cut my hair
white linens shadow
my face
a cotton veil
covers my head
black pleated wool
replaces satin

i feel sacrifice
turn to loss
like silk under glass
beauty folded
into something small
hidden, weighted down
pressed into narrow
confines of age
the will of a God
stronger than mine

we return to chapel
players in
a medieval script
i hear my name
henceforward Sister Susanne

a beautiful young sister
gasps
she's being tested
named Sr. Bartholomew

afterwards my mother asks
are you able to breathe?

community

here we are never alone
never together

working in the refectory
sr. emma breaks silence
*"why is friendship,
so normal in life,
forbidden here?"*

her question
breaks into my
solitary cell,
touches me

she finishes my work
tells me to walk
in the gardens.

biblical message

Friday night
Monsignor Farrell
white hair stooped shoulders
long black cassock
wide red sash
glasses too thick to see
young nuns missing home
former seminary prof
Biblical Theology
book of Ruth
book of Job
Genesis
Adam and Eve

Monsignor mumbles
for two hours
Job and his pain
come close
an old man
struggling with a message
none of us can hear.

promise

Sunday night
in the novitiate
Chopin Mozart Bach
music to calm
the senses
Sister Anita
finds a rhythm
like a gypsy girl
raises long skirts
taps her feet
sound beat magic
take her to a dance floor
the Beatles, Connie Francis, Elvis
can't help falling
in love with you
light of a midnight moon
stars waiting for a wish
taste of Jim's kiss
counting past a hundred
promising he'll wait.

model

she swirls
into the novitiate
wearing high heels
a blue silk dress
red lipstick
Venetia Ford
has modelled
haute couture clothes
in London Paris Rome
she begins our instruction
how to walk
like a lady
how to eat
in public
which cutlery to use
we practice walking
books balanced
on our heads
some toppling
to the floor
Venetia Ford
is still smiling
when a bell chimes

Elm St. Saints

I open
a red sewing box
kindness of neighbours
woven into patterns
warm in my hands

Mrs. Lens
cleansed my bleeding foot
changed the dressing
morning noon and night

Mrs. Hughes
measured me
for a new dress
every year of school

Mrs. Finn
took pictures on
first communion day

Miss Hudson
encouraged my parents
offered good advice
stayed for tea

Mrs. White
sent pink roses
from her shop
on graduation day
women outside a cloister
saints living on Elm St.

after dark

a sister
from my hometown
takes me aside
tells me she's leaving

she keeps seeing
a pine coffin
carried down
convent steps
a black veil
covering her face

after dark
her brother
meets her
at the laundry door
as if she
is somewhat sullied
defrocked
labelled

she wants to live
close to the sea
to sailing winds
to footprints
covered in sand

she'll send an address
to my mother

angel

sister andre
lights candles before mass
her tall thin figure
moves around the altar
like an angel
with folded wings
eyes of a stone seraph
keeping vigil
over sunken graves
beside a church

between chimes
of matins and lauds
sister andre
loses words to her prayers
wanders into a silence
even god leaves
without a whisper.

censored

a library shelf
in the novitiate
has a paperback
on marriage
the chapter on
conjugal love
sealed with
masking tape
words hidden
like full breasts
under layers
of tight binding

34

someone
has peeled back
brown tape
opening a forbidden
passage.

christmas letter

christmas morning
we gather in a classroom
exchange greetings
receive letters from home

in a silent corner
i read words
in the gaelic blessing
of my father's hand

this christmas day
mother will cook turkey
brothers and their wives
will come for dinner
a grandchild is due
early in the new year

convent rule forbids me
to hold a newborn
maternal instinct
might fill my breast
awaken desire
for a baby
i can name.

chaplain

our new chaplain
a tall fastidious man
prancing around the altar
in lordly vestments
like a high priest
bearing a papal crown

Father Boniface watches
through black rimmed bifocals
pins notes on the bulletin board,
"I have observed a nun
snipping bloomers from the garden."

someone should slip him
a pair of bloomers
and take note.

wrinkles

every monday
thirty novices work
in the laundry
a steaming mangle
fed by blistered hands
presses towels, sheets, aprons
piles of large handkerchiefs

i'm assigned
to the ironing room
father boniface has
coloured pajamas
blue, green, taupe,
lemon, plum, paisley, striped
sr. helga instructs me
to iron them wrinklefree

i struggle with the crease,
if it turns out
crooked, off-centre,
father boniface
will have bad dreams

number 764

sisters who have
professed final vows
have a laundry number
on a shelf.
every monday i
return clean clothes
to number 764
she has soft underwear
bra and panties
trimmed in lace
sweet traces
of the world,
of the feminine,
worn under a habit
by a woman.

38

art in the parlour

carerra marble halls
doors opening to
chandeliers hardwoods
tables of mahogany
plum settees
deep enough for a bishop

original oils
turn walls to art
an abbess
and her nuns
form a line

wooden steps
to a scaffold
red blade of
revolution
veiled heads
mixed with crowns
spilling into baskets
made of straw

novitiate

leaves of lazy fern
drinking filtered light
spread between
long polished tables
hardback chairs
in perfect rows

women
doubting God's call
to marriage to motherhood
female voices
making radio announcement
taking the place of men

thirty white-veiled novices
enter in silence
wait for the novice mistress
to be seated

questions end in silence
dead air

she's been on retreat
has heard a prophet
a Jesuit who teaches
the wisdom of Divine Will
in a world where
sacred order
is in disarray

nuns swimming at the lake house

large wooden structure
hidden behind fences
struggling with age

boxes of skirted
swimwear
squeamish relics
of victorian modesty
long black robes
worn over suits
to the water's edge

talking allowed
for hours and hours
swimming
walking
lawn bowling

a professed sister
complains loudly
*novices should not
be allowed here
they haven't earned
any privilege*

drowning

i swim late
in the afternoon
unsettled waters
draw me deeper
begin to pull
tempting me
to pass over
black and white nights
fading into grey mornings

the supper bell
sounds through
wind and wave,
calling

intruder

two am at the lake house
lights snap on
frantic voices
"get scissors, get knives
a man is hiding,
his footsteps sounded
like gritty sandals
scraping over wood"
sister maude thinks
she saw a shadow
near her bed
maybe he's in the cloakroom

a louder voice
"stay together
for the search"

after screams, tears, prayers
someone makes
hot chocolate
we return to bed

sister gerald awakens me
"susanne it's you
grinding your teeth!"

wedding party

on our return
from the lake
we stop
at a country church
a wedding party
gathers on the lawn
the bride
embraced in sunlight
the eyes of her bridegroom
her promise to life

excitement
starts to flow
to rise into
mardi gras sounds
glints of colour
a letting go
each of us a voyeur
crowding in

if we too are brides
called to heaven's
marriage feast,
why are we
so hungry
so thirsty
dusty pilgrims
on forbidden ground

the novice mistress stands,
silence spreads,
black and white
rules slide into place,
sisters today begins
the bride's joys
and her sorrows.

44

comfort food

every Saturday
our evening meal
a boiled egg
a tea biscuit
applesauce

atonement for sin
committed this night
by women and men

sexual sin
unnamed
silenced
even the words
arouse demons
thought
feeling
desire
carnal need

nunnery rhyme

convent silence
spreads whispers
stories of a music teacher
beautiful Sister May
who removed
her holy habit
handed in her cross
her book of prayers
walked down convent
stairs

sisters tempted to stray
remember to pray

sisters tempted to stray
remember to pray

was found strangled
maybe worse

sisters tempted to stray
remember to pray
for dear departed
Sister May

travelled to England
rented a flat
met a stranger
at a dance

silent leaving

in a darkened novitiate
i meet the novice mistress

in silence we walk
through an airless tunnel
to a creaky elevator
relic of a boarding school
whispers of young girls
up and down empty halls

we reach the attic
shadowed room lit
with one bulb
filled with trunks
angry stirring of bats

sister carlene breaks silence
pronounces a name
failed novice about
to vanish
through midnight doors
morning phantom
in chapel
at breakfast
next to me in class

we search
rows of dusty locks
together we lift
sister charlotte's trunk
as if it holds
her slender young body

breathing

47

watch

we dress the same
walk the same
think the same
keep the same rule
in the mid-sixties
a watch is permitted
a gift from family

watches begin
to appear
on young wrists
gold, gold-plated,
silver, round, oval, square

jewelry in a nunnery
unwinding pride
telling more than time

48

letters to the world

1965

a year ago
i taught school
drove a red ford falcon
sang at weddings
danced to the Beatles
"all you need is love"
celebrated Christmas
with my family

now convent walls
brick around my mind
rules become mortar
sealing cracks
as if light carries sin

father mother brothers
friends neighbours
reduced to "laity"
a lower class
in heaven's hierarchy
out of the running
for sainthood
to be addressed
in christian charity
measured in a thimble

an old sister
takes me by the arm
asks about my parents
counsels me
to write to them
often

49

visit

my uncle John
from New York
a subway engineer
walks with me
in summer gardens

he looks at me
in heavy medieval black
remembers me dancing
bright flowered dresses
of childhood
in his gentle brogue
he counsels me
to leave this place

marry a good man
have sons and daughters

his words
gather around me
like children
waiting for permission.

50

warmth

sixteen of us
sleep in single beds
under thin blankets
white cotton gowns

cold air pours through
windows open
to november winds
as if warmth
carries sin
in the comfort
of its breath
taken in
and held.

51

confession

dormitories
sixteen curtained beds
five-thirty bell
sixteen toothbrushes
break silence

chapel at six
meditation communal prayers
breakfast in silence
preparation for first vows
in the novitiate

*sisters if anyone of you
is not a virgin
you must make it known
to me
before vows*

the words
spoken by the novice mistress
fall upon us like sixteen thieves
in a sanctuary
making us tell

the young sister
in the corner bed
cries all night
her tears falling
through questions
"why?"
within days
her place at table
is empty

*"sisters, please have
the charity to pray
for one who
is no longer
with us."*

open door policy

father mark
my parish priest
meets with me
closes the door

he asks about
my health
why am i so thin
am i getting enough sleep

sister bertha
opens the door
a rule book
written in lines
around her eyes
she excuses herself
leaves the door
"ajar"
father mark
reaches for the handle
pulls it hard

says he hopes
sister bertha
didn't hurt
her nose.

epigram: no sister can be alone
    with a man, even her father,
    unless the door is left ajar.
    convent rule,no.85

53

web

in a convent parlour
a heavy lamp
rests on mahogany
casts shaded light
on dustless floors
a cushioned settee
stitched in the plum
of velvet

the molded corner
suspends a web
fine spun over a thousand years
too dark to be caught
in the eye of a young novice
preparing for
poverty chastity obedience.

first vows in a sinful world

whispers of Vatican Two
new habits
faces free of linen
hair pulled back
under a tight headpiece

vows of poverty
chastity
obedience
for one year
professed in the cathedral

vested in red
the bishop proclaims
the heroism of chastity
in a sinful world

the new headpiece clamps
over my brow
pain flattens the
bishop's words
into a string of sounds
tied in knots.

nuns' band

Arthur Dunn
a local musician
wants a nuns' band
members who will
never leave
a testimony in music

i've chosen
a brass baritone
an instrument
fitted to my lips
my fingers opening valves
freeing high bold notes
joined with trumpet
flute oboe clarinet
timpani
during practice Arthur
instructs me
to hold the baritone
as if i were holding him
he seems confused
when we all laugh.

band practice

a long hall
outside the laundry
leads to an oak staircase
rising to high-ceilinged rooms
once a girls' boarding school
heavy armoires breathe dust
harbour empty hangers
a few broken mothballs

in these rooms
we practice
hour upon hour
sister Marsha
holds her trumpet high
masters every note
plays from memory
wins a word of praise
from Arthur Dunn

butterflies

forty medieval players
crowd into a bus
leaving for Montreal
we've been invited
to perform
at Chateau Frontenac

we arrive
at a convent
set in summer sun
french speaking nuns
welcome us
serve coffee
warm butter croissants

show us through
gleaming Provençal parlours
into the library
a sister studying science
travels to India, Africa,
collects rare butterflies

pins opalescent wings
blue iridescence
untouchable,
reflecting in
polished glass

concert

at Chateau Frontenac
we play
in a convention hall
thick blue carpets
polished chandeliers
Arthur Dunn leads us
in broadway tunes
lively choral selections
ending with
the Warsaw Concerto
eighteen year old
Sr Jeanine
at the grand piano

nuns under light
on a stage
in the sixties
another small
uncovering

custody of the eyes

from the beginning
we are taught
custody of the eyes
on the street
in an office
on a bus

except for
crossing streets
eyes must be cast down

on the bus
people stare
at a young nun
carrying a black case
holding a brass baritone

if i look
into the eyes
of the other
who will i see
a young man
from teachers' college
a handsome stranger
who plays music
a jealous god
who makes me
confess?

the red dress

1967
i return to the classroom
wearing the habit
children, tired of black
asking
sister can't you wear
colour
just for one day

i see myself
before entering
a young teacher
barely nineteen
wearing a red dress
rich corduroy
tight bodice
full skirt
children in a reading circle
touching the hem
miss you look so beautiful.

61

staff room

in a core city school
i pass by the staff room
teachers drinking coffee
sharing art ideas,
before entering
i sat among them

now i eat lunch
in a small room
with the principal,
Sister Mildred
one day in November
she asks
*"Do you have a sister
or an aunt in community
who will look after you
if you become ill?"*

her question
spreads like smoke
rising from ash

lessons

mr. jones
fresh from college
teaches grade six
comes to my classroom
monday mornings
before class
i play the melody line
for his music lesson
on an upright piano
he whistles the tune
keeps it in his head

sister mildred
closes her office door

tells me mr. jones
must prepare lessons
on his own

invitation

father vincent invites
sister mildred and i
for lunch
we join him
and father francis
in a dining room
faded rose wallpaper
windows closed
shaded from sunlight
an antique lamp
with a brass cherub
glaring in the corner
like an angry eye

sister mildred
comments on the dessert
fresh cherries and sherbert
afterwards she tells me
about sister earnestine
who served a bishop
ripe red cherries
handpicked from
a convent garden
a small white worm
wrapped around
every seed

and she smiled.

bishop's mansion

saturday mornings
i drive with sister flora
to a massive residence
overlooking the river

on the second floor
neat closets of
hooded vestments
gold threaded linen
white red green
purple black

i wash a gold chalice,
the lid slips
from my fingers
spins across hardwood
stops at sister flora's
feet
her face reddens
into a wrinkled mask

she directs me
to check vestments
for spots
to iron the bishop's alb

our labour is invisible
as if angels
appear every Saturday
leave before lunch

65

wake

Sr. Dierdre
met visiting nuns
in Ireland
followed them here
with only prayers
to seal in letters
home

for every
September class
Shakespeare Browning
Blake
alive in her heart
awake on her lips

so young to die
she rests now
in the wavering light
of convent candles

no fiddlers here
to sound the dirge
no poteen poured
to quench the grief
of Irish loss

pray God
welcomes her
in the soft
of Gaelic verse
cayhe wilthu

reflections

Sr. Lionel Marie
recites her poetry
on the stage
in the gym
too much beauty
to be hidden
in convent veils

she pictures herself
in a smoke filled
coffee house
hears her voice
framing words
phrases pictures
gathered into meaning
loaves and fishes
enough to feed
a crowd

sacred book

in early May
the book of vows
is opened
on carved cherry wood
pages of calligraphy
framed in fresh cut tulips

I, Sister Pierre Marie
do solemnly take final vows
Poverty
Chastity
Obedience
sacred promises
to my divine bridegroom
whom I profess
to serve
in Christian love
until death do us meet.

my name cannot
be entered here
my hand cannot
form the words
i cannot promise
never to welcome
a husband to my bed
a child to my breast

if i leave
will i be
like Lot's wife
looking back?

giving scandal

my brother visits
he's travelled for hours
has hours to go
i suggest a walk
in the gardens
close to open gates

we walk arm in arm
talking about home
mom and dad
aging and alone,
a hand
moves convent curtains

when my brother leaves
i am chastised
by my superior
she says i may
have given public
scandal
walking arm in arm
with a man

change

a certain beauty
cannot be enclosed
in a habit

Sister Justine
knew she was allowed
to show
one inch of hair
pulled back
under the black
headpiece

on a spring morning
in 1969
she walked into chapel
strawberry blonde hair
cut into bangs

when she came back
from communion
rules scattered
like dust balls
in a breeze

Prince of Prague

the Prince of Prague
stands on his pedestal
a two-year old Christ
crown of jewels
dressed / undressed
by loving hands
silk robe
velvet cape
changed every month
colours of conquered worlds
purple red green gold
sewn by consecrated virgins
denied nuzzling baby sons
pouring mother's milk
on marble.

lock and key

Sister Angeline
said no
to the man she loved
refused the satin
of marriage
chose the wool
of convent black

years wore
sacred vows
into lines
around narrow lips

a papal pen
released her from
poverty
chastity
obedience
dispensation papers
sealed in Rome

these she kept
under the lock
of her trunk
held the key
in her hand

freedom
she could touch

if she dared

doubt

we've been counselled
directed warned
never to entertain
any thought
leading away from
convent walls
from God's holy will

some classmates
are leaving
moving into
the noisy sixties

final vows
are a year away
a thousand years
won't prepare me
i feel as if i'm alive
inside a glass coffin

monastic prayer

late in the sixties
monastic prayer
is restored
nuns standing
bowing kneeling chanting
matins compline
vespers lauds

sister walter marie
wonders why
"all this bowing and scraping?"
her words spread
across the room
like poison
spilled from a pail

leaving–from the front door

sister patrick thomas
teaches english
in the girls' academy

tells her students
she is leaving
from the front door

the next morning
three hundred girls
in blue uniforms
form a guard of honour
down an oak staircase
along marbled halls
sister patrick thomas
walks through
smiling, waving,
tossing long black hair,
wearing high heels,
a bright red miniskirt

English 101

1969-
i begin
summer university courses
English and History

the English prof
perches on a windowsill
like Peter Pan
reads passages from
William Blake
"weep weep"
choked from the throat
of a four year old,
ash of England's fire
"burning bright"

we study Huckleberry Finn
a moral decision
breaking chains
"a black man has a soul"

Professor Williams
meets with me
marks me with his eye
"failure with an A"

novel

on summer campus
i feel invisible
among so many
young eyes
my veil and cross
relics worn in daylight

restless for pages
written outside
ruled margins
i search shelves
for a novel
Hemingway, Lawrence, Joyce

a librarian
reaches for Somerset Maugham
On Human Bondage

St. Pius Convent

convent halls
becoming darker
longer
farther from God

silence shifting
moving around me
ice in a river
breaking

i ask for a move
to another city
arrive at
St. Pius Convent
with my trunk
welcomed by
Sister Simone
a superior
who believes this life
deserves some joy

we gather for
Sunday dinner
scalloped potatoes
roast chicken
garden greens
lemon pie

in table chatter
i hear
my mother singing
stirring warm pie filling
squeezed from lemons
sweetened by her Gaelic
song.

the only choice

sister simone
invites me to her table
for supper
a franciscan priest
is visiting

father alphonse
middle-aged overweight
enjoys food and wine
tells of his travels
in Canada and the U.S.
speaks of change
says a community
should not encourage
a young sister
who doubts her vocation
to stay

"every year in a convent
lessens a woman's chance of
marriage."

Sister Monique

Sister Monique prepares meals
fit for thirty priests

from her youth
a convent housekeeper
denied a cookbook
pages opening to a feast
inviting her to be seen
through all that black
a woman who
could have led
the dance
raised enough sons
to please a bishop
opened her house
to food music wine
joie de vivre

she waits for the paper
finds a French name
in the obituary
attends the wake
becomes visible
welcomed embraced
joyful visitation
like Mary and Elizabeth
before a birth

thirty day retreat

freshly ploughed fields
trails through forests
wild roses in bud
purple violets hidden
among tangled roots
oak stretching
in the sun
seeds of power
spread by squirrels

silence
in my room
at the table
in my prayers
daily meetings
with Father Thomas
sister
don't you think
God respects
your intelligence
if you
are hearing
a voice
from your heart
listen

freedom

i'm not afraid
of leaving
having no money
staying in a boardinghouse
living in a city of strangers

freedom is
lifting me above
monday to friday
taking me to weekends

coffee in a shop
blue jeans in a park

maybe

sister liam thomas
a nurse turning forty
knows i'm leaving
she wants to open
convent gates
walk away

maybe her health
won't last
maybe she'll be poor
maybe she'll be alone

maybe she'll stay.

learning to dance

opening to the promise
held in morning
sister fiona
hides long auburn hair
under black convent veils

she shows me
a pink dress
a new slip
edged in lace
holds it to herself
sashays across the room
as if her body
is learning a new dance
grace of a young goddess
answering prayer

friend

in my last year
i teach
with Lisa
a new bride
whose gentle beauty
draws children
in the yard
in the halls
in the classroom

Lisa knows
there's been a struggle
a change
asks if i'm leaving
says she'll sew
a blue dress

fabric of my
first summer

clothes

Jane
my brother's wife
offers to make
clothes for my leaving
miniskirts for summer campus
two in red
one in white
strappy sandals to match

i've grown my hair long
tied back
hidden under black
every night
i loosen the knot
feel like a bride
before a mirror
unveiling
longing for a door
to open

business

my last day
at St.Pius convent
i am summoned
into the presence
of the generalate
mother superior
with her advisors

she tells me
to be seated
there are papers
to be signed
to be witnessed
terms read
legal
final
return of my
one hundred dollar
dowry-without interest
some money to stretch
over the summer
no extensions
nothing more

i am told
not to visit
the mother house

mother superior
embraces me
christian charity

leaving

late June-1972
i stand before
a small convent mirror
remove layers of black garb
release long thick hair
hidden under chaste veils
feel silk on young
breasts hips legs
covering my body
in naked colour
for the first time
in eight hungry years

new heels sound
on winding backstairs
taking me down
to steel hinges
opening

journey

an hour later
i'm on a train for home
bright afternoon sun
conductor offering
coffee tea sandwiches
food for the journey

i return
to pre-convent days
early sixties
JFK is dead
so is my best friend
Colleen,
who carried me
over childhood years
closer than any sister
from my mother's womb
buried now
in a blue dress
sewn for graduation day

a convent on the hill
call of angelus
never clear
mother superior
asking if i own a car
telling me to
bring it here
commerce of religion
overturned

i've promised my father
my first disobedience.

89

in closing

Sister Simone
softens my leaving
tells me to keep
my cross
my book of prayers
given in a ceremony

within a week
the superior general
sends a letter
convent possessions
held by the former
Sister Susanne
must be returned

the next morning
i take a cab
to St. Pius Convent
hand Sr. Simone
a cross and a book
eight years of youth
tied together.

voice

winter is over
rains have turned
to flowers
droplets of yellow
gathering in green fields
i'm hearing a voice
calling me by name

it was always there
in convent halls
in chapel
in midnight dreams
afraid to break
a silence held sacred

summer

i stepped into summer
as i remembered it
soft butter mornings
spreading into afternoons
walking on campus
talking to a friend
fellow neophyte
she's met someone
he's staying at a cottage
takes her in a boat
to where it's deep
i wonder if he's married
if he's being fair

she says he's
a lot like Jesus
she knows his face.

first paycheck

boardinghouse address
Walter and Ida
beyond middle years
weary of empty places
around their table

my room upstairs
flowers pasted on dusty walls
wasted in the sun
single bed
covered in plaid
a desk and chair
my convent trunk
filled with books
waiting for
a September classroom
first paycheck

TABLE OF CONTENTS